Foundation Curriculum
Copyright © 2014
Written by Linda D. Washington
Illustrated by Rebeca Flott
Edited by Joyce S. Pace and Rita K. Jeffries

STORY BOOK LESSON 3
"JESUS"

Why do you think
Jesus told us to pray and say,
"Give us this day our daily bread?"

Here's a clue.
Jesus said that God sent him from heaven as the bread of life!

Listen closely to the story so you will know why Jesus is your bread of life.

Father told the first man, Adam, one thing he was not supposed to do.

Do you remember what it was?

God told Adam not to eat from the tree of the knowledge of good and evil because he would die. Adam did not believe God. Adam disobeyed his Father and sinned. Bad things like sickness and death spread to all people born from the seed of Adam. People chose to think, speak and do evil things like Adam. People thought their feelings were more important than the words of love that God spoke. They did not choose to be God's children or do things His way anymore.

The earth was not the way God made it. God had given the earth to His children to be in charge of and make into a kingdom of love. But instead the earth had become the devil's kingdom of sin, death and evil.

God called the bad things that people did sin. Sin made Father sad because God's children did not understand His love. But there was one way that Father's children could be saved from sin and know His love again.

God made many laws such as the law of sin and death. The law of sin and death caused everyone who sinned to die. The only way this law could be stopped was for someone who had no sin to die for everyone. But who had no sin on earth? And who would be willing to die for everyone?

God has no sin. He is love. God never quit loving His children. He knew that all people had sinned. So God, Himself, chose to be born on the earth, and die in your place, so that everyone who believes Him could be saved from the law of sin and death. Then people could choose to be His child, know His love, and be like Him.

This is how He did it! God has shown us three parts of Himself. One, He showed us Himself as our Father when He made us His children. Two, He showed Himself as a Holy Spirit when He breathed life into us. And three, now He will show you Himself as His own Son, Jesus, so that He can save you. He is One God in three forms, Father, Son and Holy Spirit. And His love for you never ends.

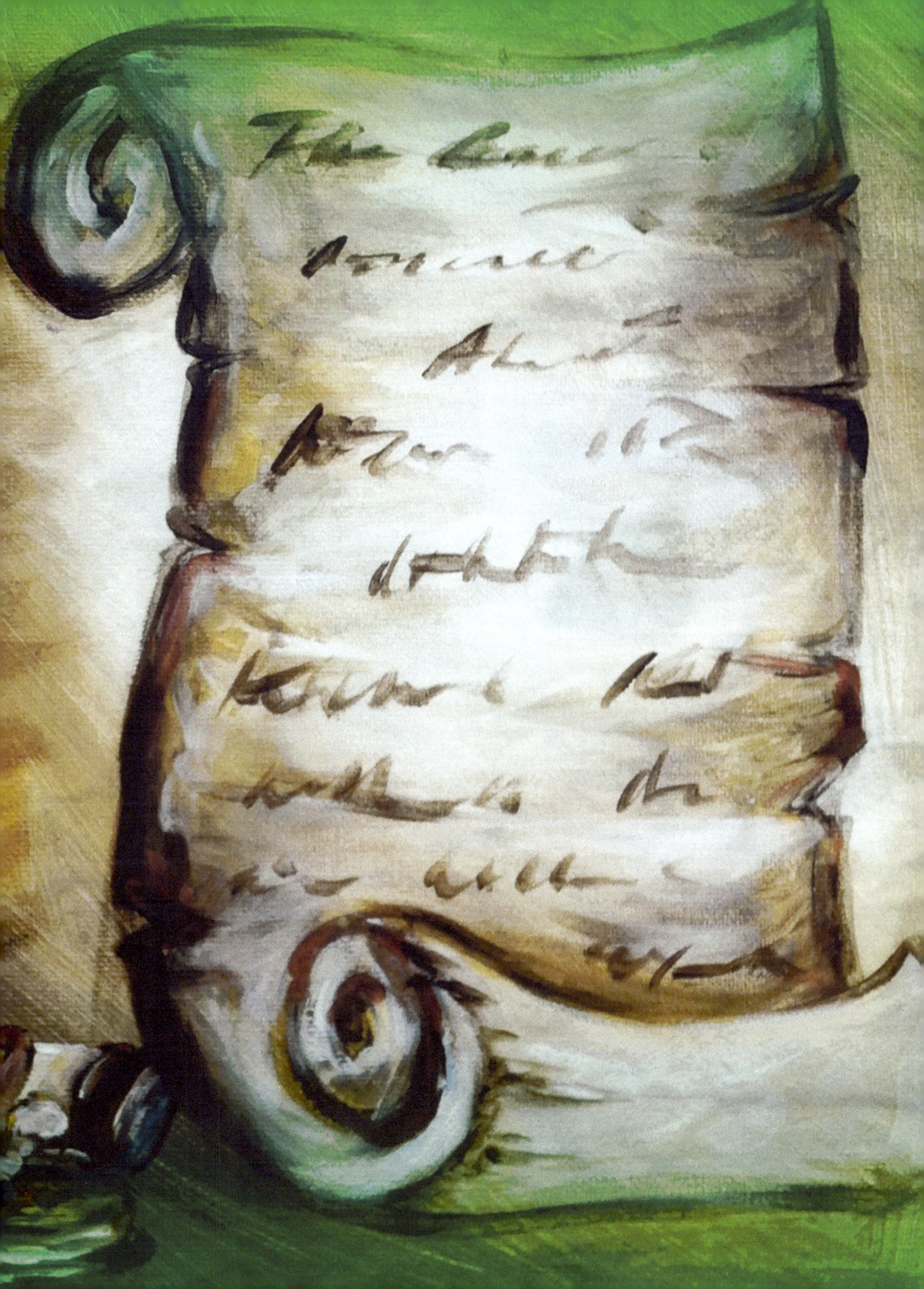

Do you remember the good seed God put inside of Adam for all people to be born from?

Sin made the seed in Adam turn bad. So heavenly Father put His good seed inside of Jesus, and Jesus was born from Father, not from Adam.

When Jesus came to earth, he did the good things that Father told him. He made sick people well. He made some dead people come back to life. He made the devil leave people alone. He told people that God was their Father and how much God loves them. But many people still did not believe Jesus and hated him.

Would you give your life and die for people in a world that hated you?

Jesus did! As a man, Jesus obeyed his Father and took your place. Some people did mean things to Jesus. They tied him up. They laughed and made fun of him. They blindfolded him. They hit him on his face and head.

People said things that were not true about him. They spit in his face and smacked the one who made them with the palm of their hand.

Again they punched him with their fists and struck him with the palms of their hands. They took off his clothes and beat his body with a whip and tore his skin open. They pushed a crown of thorns down on his head.

What do you think Jesus said to them?

He did not say a word because he loved them.

With his back and body beaten and bruised, they told him to carry a heavy wooden cross up a hill.

They hammered huge nails into his feet and hands to lock him tight onto a cross. They stood the cross up like a tree so that his body would hang and bleed until his body died.

Every sickness, disease and sadness from sin went into his body so that whoever believes he died for them never has to be sick or sad again. His face and body had more marks on it than any person that ever lived. Jesus did not look human anymore.

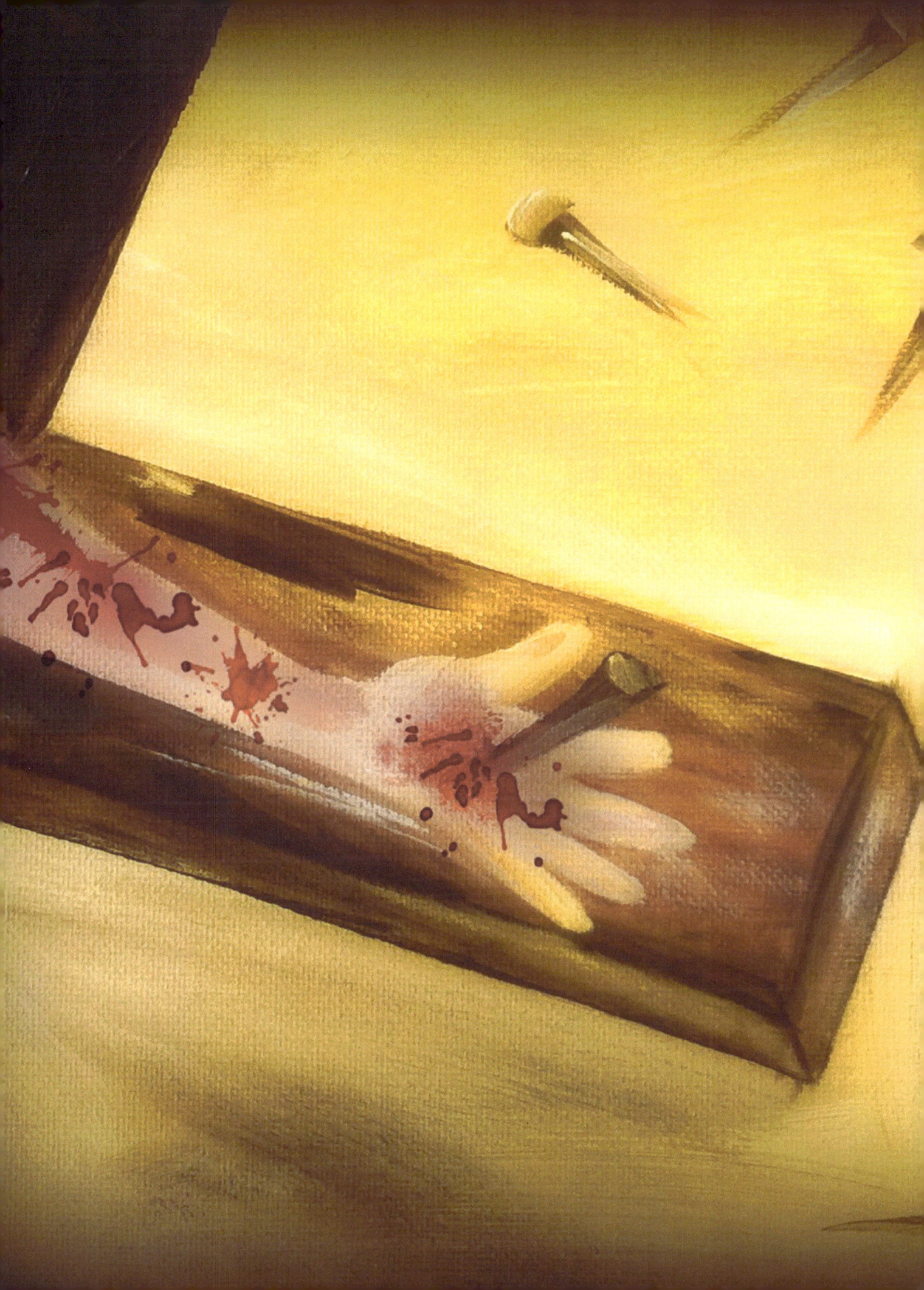

Jesus prayed to his Father as he hung on the cross dying. He said to his Father, "**FORGIVE THEM**, because they do not know what they are doing." People watched him hurt for six hours on the cross before his body died.

Then Jesus cried with a loud voice, and let his spirit leave his body, "FOR YOU!"

How does this make you feel?

When his spirit left his body, Jesus went into a deep, dark, scary place called hell. Jesus was not afraid! Satan and all his demons thought they had won because they tricked the people into killing the Son of God. **But guess what happened?**

Jesus rose up with BIG power to show them that God is the boss. POW! BAM! The devil didn't know what hit him. Jesus wrecked the devil and made his demons run. He took the keys of hell and death from satan. **JESUS WON!**

He beat the devil and his demons for you and everyone born on earth.

JESUS IS OUR SUPER HERO! Let's thank him. Thank you Jesus! Let's cheer and clap for Jesus. YAY Jesus!

Let's thank Father for sending Jesus. Thank You Father! We love You!

FATHER AND JESUS DID IT!

Jesus let His body die, and his blood covered the sins of every person that would ever be born on earth.

Do you think Father let His Son stay in hell?

No! Father lifted Jesus up from hell by His power of Holy Spirit.

When Jesus returned from hell, he told people about the kingdom of God. Jesus had finished everything his Father told him to do. It was time for Jesus to go home to live with his Father again. Jesus was caught up and a cloud carried him towards heaven.

Now God has forgiven everyone. But Father is waiting for you to tell Him with your words that you believe Jesus, and you want to be born again in your spirit as His child.

Do you know what it means to be "Born Again" as a child of God?

All people were born the first time from the seed in Adam.

Do you remember what sin did to Adam's seed?

Sin made the seed in Adam turn bad. Jesus said that your spirit must be "Born Again" by the good seed that Father put in him. To be "Born Again" means that you can choose to be born a second time in your spirit by the good seed in Jesus. Then you can be a child of God, like Jesus, in your spirit.

Close your eyes.
Listen to the questions.
Then raise your hand up to answer yes.
Or leave your hand down to answer no.

Would you like to be "Born Again" in your spirit with the good seed that heavenly Father put in Jesus?

Remember hands down for no, and hands up for yes.

Keep your eyes closed, and answer these questions from your heart.

Do you want to stop doing bad things and love like heavenly Father?

Do you believe that Jesus died for your sins so you can know the love of Father?

Do you believe that heavenly Father raised Jesus from the dead by His power of Holy Spirit?

If you raised or kept your hand up to show that you truly believe Father and Jesus, SPEAK WORDS from your heart now and TELL HIM you believe.

Open your eyes. If you said words from your heart to God that you believe Jesus, you have been "Born Again" from the good seed in Jesus.

You are heavenly Father's child of love, like Jesus! Welcome to God's family of love!

Let's thank Father and Jesus.
Thank You Father!
Thank You Jesus!
Thank You for dying for me!
Thank You for forgiving me for my sins!
Thank You Father for making me Your child!
I love You!

GOD HAS TWO GIFTS FOR YOU!

Before Jesus went back to heaven, he asked Father to give you gifts. Two of these gifts are His Holy Spirit and God's special language called tongues.

Do you remember that Holy Spirit is God also?

It was by the power of God's Holy Spirit that Jesus healed the sick and made the devil leave people alone. The power of God's Holy Spirit lifted Jesus up from hell. Father wants His Holy Spirit to live in you just like He is in Jesus and Father.

Holy Spirit will help you remember to choose to do what is right and good. Holy Spirit will help you to speak to God in His special language called tongues.

Father wants you to receive His gift of Holy Spirit to help you love like Jesus, and to have His power in you, to do good things on earth for Him!

Would you like to receive God's gift of Holy Spirit?

If you spoke words from your heart and said you believe Jesus, then you can choose to pray and ASK Father to receive Holy Spirit. And Father will give you Holy Spirit! Or you can pray these words:

"Father,
I want to be like You and Jesus!
I want to show Your love to everyone.
Will You give me Your Holy Spirit?
I receive Your Holy Spirit inside of me.
I know Holy Spirit is with me now and forever!
Thank You Father!
Welcome Holy Spirit!!!"

Father knows that sometimes you don't know what to pray, but Holy Spirit has a special language of God called tongues that helps you pray God's will.

Would you like to speak the language of God?

If you want to speak in tongues, don't try to think of words to say, just speak. Holy Spirit will do the rest. Open your mouth. Trust God. And begin to speak the sounds that come out of your mouth. You can stop whenever you want.

Let's just talk to our Father in tongues now! Find a secret place to be alone and talk to your Father. Then listen and hear what God says to you. You can talk to your Father in your language or in tongues whenever you choose.

YOUR FATHER IN HEAVEN LOVES YOU!

The Purpose of the Foundation Curriculum

To firmly establish God's truth in each child's heart early in life so they will understand and know God's love and choose to live fully in the victory that Jesus Christ has already won.

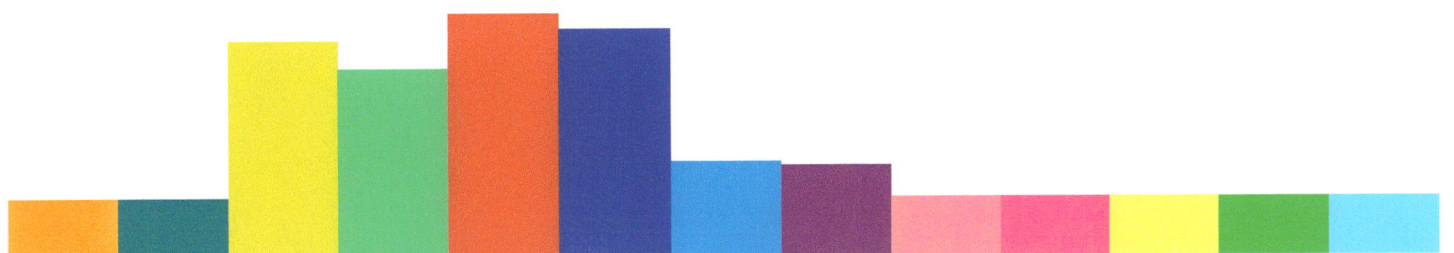

The Goals

To show God's children his love, their true identity as children of God, their authority and power in Christ Jesus, their helper Holy Spirit, and how to pray to their Father in heaven.

JESUS

Story Book Lesson 3

The Objectives to understand from "Jesus" are:

1. Sin had made the seed in Adam turn bad.

2. People did not believe Father.

3. Father had made laws that He would not break.

4. The devil was killing and making people sick.

5. Father still wanted His children to love like Him.

6. Father, Son (Jesus), and Holy Spirit is One God.

7. Jesus was born on earth into a body by the good seed of God, not Adam.

8. Holy Spirit helped Jesus show love, like Father.

9. Jesus let people hurt and kill His body.

10. Jesus' Spirit went to hell for us.

11. Jesus defeated the devil.

12. Jesus is our Super Hero!

13. Father raised Jesus from the dead by Holy Spirit.

14. Jesus went back to heaven to be with His Father.

15. You can pray from your heart and be Born-Again by the good seed in Jesus.

16. You can pray and receive Holy Spirit to help you to love, like Jesus.

17. With Holy Spirit you can pray directly to Father in His special language of tongues.

P.A.C.E.
Products and Activities
for Christian Education

For Free Follow-Up Activities to Reinforce This Story Book Lesson Please Visit
www.ABC-Jesus.com

Biblical quotes were from different versions of the holy Bible.

www.ingramcontent.com/pod-product-compliance
Lightning Source LLC
Chambersburg PA
CBHW040231070426
42447CB00030B/99